DAD

JOKES

◇◇◇◇◇◇◇◇◇◇◇◇◇◇◇◇◇◇◇◇◇◇◇◇◇◇◇◇

Exceptionally Bad
Dad Jokes

◇◇◇◇◇◇◇◇◇◇◇◇◇◇◇◇◇◇◇◇◇◇◇◇◇◇◇◇

The
Terribly Good
Dad jokes
Series
NO.2

FROM _ _ _ _ _ _ _ _ _ _

Copyright © DAD JOKES (Exceptionally Bad Dad Jokes) All rights reserved.
This book or any portion thereof
may not be reproduced or used in any manner whatsoever
without the express written permission of the publisher
except for the use of brief quotations in a book review.
Printed Worldwide
First Printing, 2019

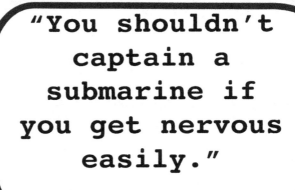